FOOD
and Farming

by Andy Tang

PEARSON

Scott
Foresman

What You Already Know

Just like animals, plants have different parts that work to keep them alive. For example, the leaves are responsible for providing the plant with food. Unlike animals, plants make their own food. Their leaves do this through a process called photosynthesis. Photosynthesis is when a plant uses sunlight to turn carbon dioxide and water into oxygen and sugar. The plant can either use the sugar for food, or store it for later. It also turns the sugar into a material called cellulose, which it uses to build and repair itself.

The stems of some plants contain two special tissues called xylem and phloem. Plants that have these tissues are called vascular plants. Xylem carries water and minerals to the plant's leaves. Phloem carries sugar from the leaves to the rest of the plant.

photosynthesis in a leaf

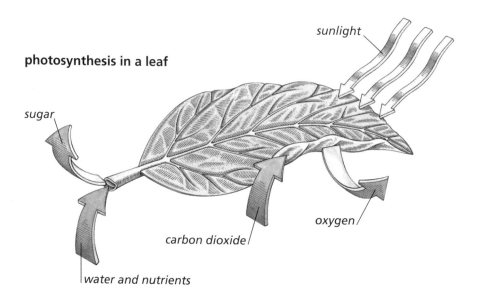

sunlight

sugar

oxygen

carbon dioxide

water and nutrients

All plants must reproduce, or make new plants. Some do this with flowers. Flowers contain pollen, which is held in the stamen. For the plant to reproduce, the pollen must get to the pistil, which contains the plant's egg cells. This process is called pollination. Sometimes pollination is done by an insect, like a bee. Sometimes it is done by wind or water. The egg and the pollen then form a new plant, or embryo. The embryo is protected inside a seed.

Some plants do not need pollination to reproduce. They release cells called spores that grow into new plants.

Seeds and spores are released by their parent plants and land in the soil, where they begin to grow. They contain chemicals called growth hormones that tell them how fast to grow. When a plant grows in a certain direction it is called a tropism. Examples of tropisms are when a plant stretches toward the sky to get more sunlight or reaches down into the ground to find more water.

You already know about how plants work and what goes on inside them. Now we'll learn about an important use people have for plants—food!

Introduction

Did you know that most of the fruits and vegetables that we eat are really parts of plants? These parts include seeds, flowers, fruits, tubers, roots, stems, and leaves. But why do we need these as part of a healthy and balanced diet? Is it because they taste good? Or is it because they contain vitamins and minerals and are good sources of energy? Read on to find out.

Most fruits and vegetables are grown on farms and orchards. While early farmers planted their crops by hand, modern farming is done with machines. Today's farmers use weather reports to decide when to plant their crops. After the crops are harvested, they can be driven directly to markets. Or they can be sent to processing plants to be made into other food products.

Seeds

We use the seeds from several kinds of plants in our food. The seeds of cereal grains, such as wheat, barley, oats, rice, rye, and maize, are used in many foods. These foods include bread, breakfast cereals, pasta, and flour. Cereal grains belong to the grass family. Beans, peas, peanuts, and soybeans are also seeds. They come from plants in the legume family, and have high nutritional values.

The seeds from the wheat plant are ground into flour, which is used in making bread.

Vegetable oils are made from seeds. They are used for cooking in many parts of the world. The seeds from plants such as corn, peanuts, soybeans, and sunflowers are used to make these oils. Vegetable oils are also used in margarine, salad dressing, and vegetable shortening. Pepper, mustard, and dill are seeds that are used to make spices. Do you ever enjoy hot cocoa or see adults drinking coffee? Both of these drinks are made from seeds!

Sunflower seeds are used to make cooking oil.

Rice

Rice is one of the most commonly eaten foods in the world. Like other cereal grains, rice is a member of the grass family. But unlike wheat, oats, and maize, rice grows best in warm, wet climates. Countries such as China, India, and Vietnam grow most of the world's rice.

Rice is usually grown in fields that have been flooded with water. Banks of earth called paddies enclose the fields to keep them flooded. Rice can either be grown by hand, by machine, or by both. In many Asian countries, oxen or water buffaloes are used to pull plows.

Rice plants are a kind of grass.

To plant rice, farmers usually grow seedlings and transplant them to a flooded field. This saves time and makes weeding easier. A modern way of planting uses machines called drills that can place seeds directly into the soil.

Rice fields are drained before they are harvested. To harvest rice by hand, farmers cut the stalks with sickles, tie the stalks in bundles, and dry them in the sun. The next step is threshing, which separates the grain from the rest of the plant. Machines called combines can harvest and thresh rice in one step.

Harvested rice is processed in mills, where it is cleaned and hulled. The hull is the hard covering of the rice kernel, or grain. The hulls can't be eaten. Machines called shellers remove the hulls from the grain. Then the rice is packaged for sale.

People all over the world eat rice.

9

Corn

Corn is one of the world's most important food crops. It has a high nutritional value and many different uses. Corn contains starch, which makes it a good source of energy. Corn is used in foods such as cereals, cooking oil, margarine, and salad dressing. Corn's non-food uses include building materials, fuels, cloth, and medicines.

Corn is a member of the grass family. It is grown in many different parts of the world, including Mexico, China, and France. The United States grows most of the world's corn.

Corn grows best in loam, a type of soil made up of sand and clay. Corn's growing season, from planting to harvesting, may begin as early as April and end as late as October.

Before planting corn, farmers plow their fields with deep furrows, or ruts. Seeds may be planted by hand or with machines called row planters.

The harvesting of corn is usually done with a machine called a corn combine. This machine can pick the ears, remove the husks, and shell and clean the corn in one step. The combine allows more corn to be harvested by fewer workers.

Corn can be eaten all sorts of ways—in a taco shell or right off the cob!

Fruits and Flowers

We like to eat fruits such as apples, oranges, and strawberries because they taste good. They give us quick energy because many of them have lots of natural sugar. Fruits such as oranges also contain vitamin C, which is very good for us.

Fruits are an important part of a balanced diet.

But what makes a fruit a fruit? Did you know that tomatoes, cucumbers, and most nuts are really fruits? Botanists, scientists who study plants, define a fruit as the part of a flowering plant that covers the seeds. Horticulturalists, people who grow plants, have a different definition. They only count soft plant parts from perennials as fruits. A perennial is a plant that lives for more than two years. To a horticulturalist, a nut is not a fruit because it is very hard. A tomato is not a fruit to a horticulturalist because tomato plants only live for one season.

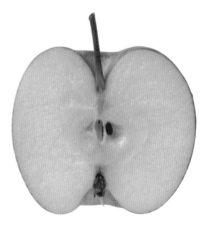

You can tell an apple is a fruit because it has seeds.

Horticulturalists classify fruits by where they grow. There are three groups of fruits. Temperate fruits, such as apples, grow in places with changing seasons and moderate temperatures. Subtropical fruits, such as oranges, grow in warmer areas. Bananas and other tropical fruits grow where it is very hot.

cherry blossom

Botanists classify fruits too. They divide fruits into simple fruits and compound fruits. As we said before, fruits grow from the part of a flower that holds the seeds. This part is called the ovary. Simple fruits grow from single ovaries. Apples, oranges, tomatoes, and cherries are all simple fruits. Compound fruits grow from two or more ovaries in a bunch. They include raspberries, strawberries, and pineapples.

Fruits come from the part of a plant's flower that contains its seeds.

Fruit or Vegetable

Vegetables are an important part of a healthy diet. They give us vitamins A, B, and K, as well as the minerals riboflavin and thiamine.

But what exactly is a vegetable? Most scientists define vegetables as parts of herbaceous plants. Herbaceous plants have leafy, green stems, unlike trees or shrubs.

Horticulturalists define vegetables differently. They only count annuals, or plants that live for only one season, as vegetables. You probably think of watermelons as fruit. But horticulturalists think of them as vegetables because they are annuals.

zucchini

Different vegetables grow in different climates. Sweet corn grows best in places with wet summers. Cool summers are best for growing lettuce. Places with colder weather are great for potatoes.

chili peppers

Look at the fruits and vegetables to the right. Which are fruits? Which are vegetables?

orange

During the winter, it is too cold to grow vegetables in the northern parts of the United States. In the past, people in these parts of the country had trouble getting fresh vegetables in the winter. But now vegetables can be grown where it's warmer and shipped very fast by refrigerated truck. This way, the whole country can have fresh vegetables all year. Some of the places that supply the rest of the country with vegetables include California and Florida.

tomatoes

pumpkin

eggplant

grapes

Flower Food

Have you eaten any flower buds lately? You have if you've eaten any broccoli, cauliflower, or artichokes. Broccoli and cauliflower plants have thick clusters of flower buds called heads. Only the buds of an artichoke can be eaten. Other flower buds that we eat include spices such as clove and saffron.

cauliflower

Fruit Farming

Almost all fruit grows on plants with woody stems, such as trees, bushes, and woody vines. Apples, oranges, and cherries are some of the fruits that grow on trees. Many small fruits, such as raspberries, grow on bushes. Grapes grow on woody vines. Since fruit plants are perennials, they don't have to be replanted each year. Many will keep producing fruit for fifty years or more!

Unlike most other crops, fruit plants are not grown from seeds. Farmers know that people pay more for fruit when each piece looks like all the others. Plants grown from seeds are a bit like children; they don't always look like their parents. So farmers have different ways of growing fruit. For trees, they take a bud from a tree that produces good fruit and join it to the roots and stem of another tree. This is called grafting. For other plants, they can use cuttings. Cuttings are plant stems that turn into new plants when placed into water or wet soil.

Fruits that come from graftings and cuttings usually grow in a way that horticulturalists expect them to. But sometimes their growers get a surprise. For example, let's look at a type of apple called the Red Delicious. If you have ever seen these apples, you know that they are bright red.

cherries

plums

But Delicious apples were not always this color. At one time they were light colored and striped. Then some Delicious trees began to grow apples that were bright red. This sort of unexpected change is called a mutation. Horticulturalists can take advantage of mutations to grow new and better kinds of fruit.

Roots, Bulbs, and Stems

A vegetable is any part of a plant that we eat that is not a fruit. These parts include roots, bulbs, and stems.

Many of the vegetables we eat are plant roots. Carrots, turnips, beets, and radishes are all root vegetables. Some, such as carrots and radishes, are large, main roots that grow straight down. These are called taproots. Other root vegetables, such as potatoes, come from roots that branch and grow sideways through the ground. These are called fibrous roots.

Carrots are taproots— large roots that grow straight down.

Turnips are another root that people like to eat.

Onions and garlic are plant parts known as bulbs. A bulb is made up of a bunch of thick leaves growing close together around a short stem. Most bulbs grow underground, with only their tops sticking out.

Another plant part we eat is the stem. Some stem vegetables are asparagus, bamboo shoots, and celery.

Did you know that a potato is really a special kind of stem called a tuber? Tubers are thick stems that grow underground and have buds. These buds grow into new plants. You may have heard of potato buds being called "eyes."

Onions and garlic are bulbs. You can see the layers of thick leaves that make up the cut onion.

Potatoes

Potatoes are the most widely eaten and grown vegetables in the world. Every year, millions of tons of potatoes are grown in countries such as China, Russia, and the United States. They are a good source of vitamins such as niacin, thiamine, and riboflavin, as well as the minerals calcium and iron. They can be boiled, baked, fried, or mashed.

The tubers of the potato plant are made up of layers. The outer layer, or skin, is called the periderm. Underneath the periderm is the cortex, which stores protein and starch. The third layer is called the vascular ring. It transports starch from the plant's stem and leaves. The pith, or the center of the tuber, is made mostly of water.

Potato plants usually have several stems that grow above the ground. Their leaves are rough and green. The plant's flowers can be white, pink, or purple.

tractor plowing field

Instead of planting seeds, potato farmers usually plant whole tubers or pieces of tubers. The whole tubers are called seed potatoes, and the pieces are called seedpieces. The eyes of these tubers or pieces grow into new plants.

Like corn, potatoes grow best in loam. They are grown in every state in the United States, but they do best in places with temperatures between 60° and 70° Fahrenheit. Cooler states, such as Idaho and Washington, grow most of our potatoes.

The part of the potato plant that we eat is a thick stem called the tuber.

Leaves

Vegetables such as lettuce, spinach, and cabbage come from the leaves of plants. Leafy vegetables can be eaten cooked, but they are also good when eaten raw.

Did you know that celery and rhubarb are leaves too? They are the stalks of leaves, called petioles. Petioles are the part of the leaf that attaches it to a plant's stem.

Leaves have uses other than for food. Leaves from tea plants are used to make tea. Seasonings such as parsley, sage, and thyme come from leaves. Peppermint and spearmint leaves are used as natural flavorings.

From roots to bulbs and from stems to leaves, we rely on different kinds of plants for food. It would be hard to imagine a healthy diet that did not include plant parts. Fruits and vegetables contain vitamins and minerals that we need to live. Thanks to modern farming and shipping, we can have the fresh fruit and vegetables we need all year round, no matter where we live.

cabbage

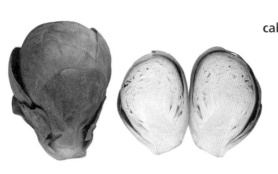

When you cut a sprout in half you can see its leaves.

Glossary

botanist a scientist who studies plants

horticulturalist a person whose job is to grow plants

legume plants such as beans that produce edible seeds inside edible pods

loam a mixture of clay soil and sandy soil

nutritional value how well a food provides the things we need for a healthy diet

perennial a plant that lives for more than two growing seasons

petiole the part of a leaf that attaches it to a plant's stem

shortening a fat used to make baked foods light and fluffy

e a tool with a short handle and a curved blade; used for cutting grass or grain

a thick stem of a plant that grows underground and has buds

Glossary

botanist   a scientist who studies plants

horticulturalist   a person whose job is to grow plants

legume   plants such as beans that produce edible seeds inside edible pods

loam   a mixture of clay soil and sandy soil

nutritional value   how well a food provides the things we need for a healthy diet

perennial   a plant that lives for more than two growing seasons

petiole   the part of a leaf that attaches it to a plant's stem

shortening   a fat used to make baked foods light and fluffy

sickle   a tool with a short handle and a curved blade; used for cutting grass or grain

tuber   a thick stem of a plant that grows underground and has buds